The
RADIANT
PRINCESS

COOMBE BOOKS

On July 29th 1981, Prince Charles, the heir apparent to the throne of Great Britain and Northern Ireland, married a blushing English beauty, Lady Diana Spencer. The marriage was held on a beautiful summer's day at St Paul's Cathedral in the heart of Prince Charles' future capital and was one of the most public weddings in Britain's history. Over half a million people lined the procession route, waving flags, banners and cuddly toys. But the vast crowds had to vie for space with dozens of camera crews, whose television networks were broadcasting the event live to an audience which numbered in the hundreds of millions.

But it was not only the wedding ceremony which was conducted in public; the wooing was also carried out in the full glare of world-wide publicity. For years, the problem of who Prince Charles was going to marry had featured prominently in the gossip columns of the world's newspapers; his succession of girlfriends and companions had led to numerous articles and widespread, popular speculation. However, it was not until the autumn of 1980 that the press started to take an interest in the teenage daughter of Earl Spencer, who was being seen in the company of Prince Charles.

Somehow, the press learnt that this time the inevitable rumours of marriage might be more than just rumours. They began to hound the future Princess, waiting outside her flat, or near the kindergarten where she worked, hoping for a photograph and perhaps a comment. Although this must have been a great strain on the young Lady Diana, she remained tight-lipped about her relationship with the Prince. From the point of view of newspaper editors, she had almost lost her news-appeal when, on the 24th of February 1981, the Palace proclaimed "It is with the greatest of pleasure that the Queen and the Duke of Edinburgh announce the betrothal of their beloved son the Prince of Wales to the Lady Diana Spencer, daughter of the Earl Spencer and the Hon Mrs Shand Kydd".

The speculation was over and arrangements for the wedding could get under way. Lady Diana at once moved in with the Queen Mother at Clarence House. Here, she was to learn the art and science of being a member of the Royal Family, perhaps the most difficult aspect of the marriage from Diana's point of view.

Despite the enormous amount of publicity engendered by the romance and the wedding, the couple managed to keep their honeymoon destination secret as they cruised around the Mediterranean aboard the *Britannia*. After their return, the affairs of State took over once again and the couple went on a short tour of Charles' Principality. Despite the occasional disturbance from Welsh Nationalists, the tour was a resounding success and the Welsh people took their new Princess to their hearts.

The Princess of Wales has become a leader of fashion, especially since the wedding. She has not allowed herself to be dictated to by the Palace officials as to what is acceptable and what is not. This independence of spirit has sometimes resulted in dreadful mistakes but, on the whole, Diana's choice of clothes has been excellent. Perhaps the most instantly recognisable feature of her fashion preferences are the pie-frill necklines which are often seen on her blouses and dresses.

Across the world, fashion designers watch the Princess of Wales for her latest innovation and the public reaction to it. Ever since her first official engagement, when she arrived in a revealing black gown, her fashions have attracted attention from the world's press for their daring and, for a Royal personage, unorthodox air.

It is not only her clothes and fashions which have brought the wind of change into Royal circles; her fresh approach to the duties of Royalty has been noticed and appreciated wherever she goes. This was nowhere more true than on the recent Royal Tours of Australia, New Zealand and Canada. The Royal Walkabout, initiated by the Queen in 1970, was brought to new heights by the Prince and Princess of Wales.

There can be no doubt that this was due, in large part, to the Princess' charm, love of children and her very prescence. It seemed as if everyone was eager to meet the new Princess and offer her bunches of flowers. The Princess, herself, always found time to speak to people in the crowd, especially to the children. This, almost invariably, made the schedule run late, but nobody seemed to mind; it was just that the Prince and Princess were so keen to meet everyone.

Even during her days as a kindergarten teacher, Diana's love of children was apparant and since the birth of Prince William this trait has become more noticeable. The prescence of Prince William on the Australian Tour was a break with Royal Tradition which was surely due to Princess Diana's influence.

There can be no doubt that the young Princess is the most popular member of the Royal Family to arrive on the scene for some time and, if present events are anything to go by, she should remain a firm favourite with the public for many years to come.

During their tours, Charles and Diana make a point of participating in local culture. On 18th June, during their 1983 visit to Canada, the Royal Couple visited Charlo (previous pages). Among those lucky enough to meet the Prince and Princess were a group of Micmac Indian children, dressed in traditional garb. When in Australia, the visiting couple climbed part of the way up Ayer's Rock before descending to watch the sun set over this famous desert landmark (these pages).

Though the year was barely a quarter of the way through its course, the ball at Sydney's Wentworth Hotel was declared the greatest social event of the year even before it happened. Crowds gathered outside, while the privileged few danced inside. The entrance of the Prince and Princess certainly justified all the excitement. Diana appeared dressed in a graceful, mid-blue evening gown, complete with diamond necklace and earrings. Though the Prince's dancing seemed short on style, the Princess and everyone else seemed to enjoy it.

On 21st June, Prince William's birthday, the Royal Couple were in Ottawa and before starting official engagements they phoned home to hear "a few little squeaks" from their son. (Previous pages) the Princess at St John.

In Canada (previous pages) the Princess wore some delightful summer outfits. Particularly at Summerside (page 17) where a local school band played a welcome to the couple. Earlier, in New Zealand, Charles and Diana visited Queen Elizabeth Park. Here they planted trees near the oaks planted by the previous Prince of Wales, in 1920, and Prince Charles' grandfather, then Duke of York, in 1927. Once again, the Royal walkabout was dominated by small children presenting gifts to their Princess, some of whom (facing page below) went to considerable lengths.

"Dress semi-formal, Klondike Days", said the invitations for an evening's entertainment in Edmonton, and Prince Charles and his lady were game enough to comply. He turned up in frock-coat and side-creased trousers, waistcoat and cravat, spats and a silver-topped cane; she wore a whaleboned silk and lace dress with bustle and train, and long, lace-up boots. There was a Gold-Rush-style music-hall show in which the Royal "couple of limeys" linked arms, sang and swayed to old-time songs.

Britannia sailed into Saint John to begin the Royal visit to New Brunswick on 17th June 1983. Prince Charles called the town "St John's", but was soon forgiven. (Facing page) the Princess in Canberra.

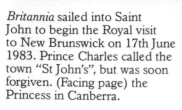

In New Zealand, the participation of the Royal Couple in the ancient Maori ceremony of rubbing noses, was almost as popular as the inclusion of Prince William on the visit.

Wherever the Princess accompanied her husband in Canada, she was an instant success; whether it was at official engagements (previous and following pages) or meeting the crowds, (this page) at Ottawa and (facing page) at Carbonear.

A shimmering, lilac gown and a bouquet from a young ballerina marked an evening out at St James' Theatre where the Royal Couple saw *Coppelia*.

The Princess' clothes throughout the Royal tour of Australia were a constant source of interest and joy to the crowds and press alike. The outfit the Princess wore on 7th April to visit Fremantle Hospital was, everyone agreed, the best so far. A stylish, deep pink dress with white spots, it was perfectly complemented by a matching pill-box hat with a large, rippling bow at the side. The Princess' outfit at Bunbury, the following day, was appreciated by all the 13,000 schoolchildren who turned out to see her.

The flamenco style hat which had served the Princess so well at Bridgewater, where Prince Charles brought "the belated gratitude of the late King George III for your unswerving loyalty", on 16th June (facing page) was brought out again at Carbonear. On this, their last day in Newfoundland, the Princess chose to wear the hat with a completely different outfit.

After a performance at
Melbourne's Concert Hall, the
Royal Couple met the artistes,
together with members of the
Victorian Cabinet and dozens of
other distinguished guests. It
was difficult to deny that the
Princess, with her spectacular
long, pink dress was, as so
often during such visits, the
star of the show.

The 14th June, the historic day the Prince and Princess of Wales arrived in Canada, was an occasion for flag waving and cheering, but the Princess stole the show with her outfit in the Canadian national colours (facing page). Later in the tour, she dispensed with a hat for an evening of music at Montague (this page). (Overleaf) Klondike Days.

The red colour scheme favoured by the Princess during a walkabout at Edmonton (overleaf) was continued when the Royal Couple attended a farewell banquet at Government House. Diana glowed in a gorgeous red gown and the Spencer tiara, while Prince Charles looked as smart as ever.

The Princess' dresses for formal occasions during the Australian and New Zealand tours varied from the romantically flouncy (this page) to the thoroughly modern and elegant (facing page). But wherever she went, she looked stunning.

Though rain and bad weather dogged much of the tour of Canada in 1983, as (opposite), the majority of events escaped the worst of the weather. During a tree-planting ceremony at City Hall Charlottetown (this page) 5,000 people turned out to cheer.

Prince Charles' first Father's Day as a father came while he and his wife were visiting Canada, and everyone wanted to know what presents he had received. Whatever presents the Princess had given her husband, enough were offered at St Andrews almost to sink the *Britannia.* Among those for Prince William was a small canoe which, according to his father, "he will be able to play with in his bath", and some fishing flies for Prince Charles. "If I'm not successful with them I can play with them in the bath as well," he joked. After the walkabout, the Royal Couple lunched at the Algonquin Hotel before leaving as they had come – by barge.

A tribal canoe carried the Royal Couple to Waitangi, the site of the treaty of 1840, during their visit to New Zealand. Prince Charles' pleas for preserving traditions seemed superfluous as in one ceremony the Princess received a jade fertility necklace.

While his parents were gallivanting around New Zealand, Prince William of Wales stayed at Government House in Auckland, where he was kept busy playing with the toys given to him in Australia. It was here, on St George's Day, that the Royal Couple agreed to bring him out for a photo-session. It was almost as if he knew it was his own show. He did everything they said he could, and more. He crawled almost as soon as they set him on the mat, showed a few of his seven gleaming teeth, and pulled up one edge of the mat to inspect its underside.

First published in Great Britain by Colour Library Books Ltd.
© 1983 Illustrations: Keystone Press Agency, London.
© 1983 Text: Colour Library Books, Guildford, Surrey, England.
Display and text filmsetting by Acesetters Ltd., Richmond, Surrey, England.
Printed and bound in Barcelona, Spain.
ISBN 0 86283 117 2